9/12

How The Rosh Hashanah Challah Became Round

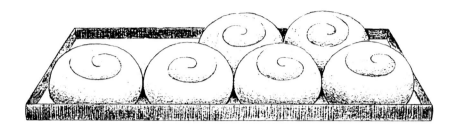

How The Rosh Hashanah Challah Became Round

By Sylvia B. Epstein
Illustrated by Hagit Migron

gefen
publishing house
JERUSALEM • NEW YORK

Photo Typeset: Gefen Publishing House, Ltd.
Illustrator: Hagit Migron
Cover Design: Helen Twena

ISBN Hard Cover: 978-965-229-095-3
ISBN Soft Cover: 978-965-229-479-1

Edition   15 14 13 12 11 10 9 8

Gefen Publishing House, Ltd.   Gefen Books
6 Hatzvi St.   600 Broadway
Jerusalem 94386, Israel   Lynbrook, NY 11563, USA
972-2-538-0247   516-593-1234
orders@gefenpublishing.com   orders@gefenpublishing.com

www.gefenpublishing.com

Printed in Israel   *Send for our free catalogue*

To David

Joseph Mordechai was his name but everyone called him Yossi. Yossi lived long, long ago in a little town far off across the sea. Yossi was the oldest of his four brothers and sisters and he liked being the oldest. He told his brothers and sisters, "I'm the only one who's big enough to help Papa. You're all too small!"

Yossi's father was the baker for the little town and all the housewives came to his bakery to buy bread for their families. Yossi was proud to be his father's helper. They baked shiny, light brown loaves of bread. They baked crusty, dark brown loaves of bread.

The day before the Sabbath or the High Holidays was always a special day in the bakery. No shiny, light brown loaves. No crusty, dark brown loaves. On that day only one kind of bread. It was long and braided; golden on the outside and white inside. It was a challah!

One special day began like every other day. Yossi and his father put on their sparkling, white aprons. Into the tub went the flour. Thump! Squeeze! Thump! Squeeze! Yossi and his father kneaded the dough. Then, ever so neatly, Yossi's father braided the dough into long, pointed challahs. Soon they were ready to go into the oven.

Yossi picked up the great pan loaded with challahs. He felt very important as he started down the stairs to the oven. He sang a song:

"Yossi, Yossi, son of the baker,
He's the bread and challah maker.
Thump! Squeeze! Knead the dough!
He makes challah white as snow."

Yossi was so pleased with his new song that he forgot to watch for the bump on the top step. Thunk!..... Bang!...... Bumpity!..... Bump! Yossi tripped! The pan slid out of his hands and every single one of the Rosh HaShanah challahs rolled down the stairs.

Yossi couldn't say a word. Big, salty tears ran down his cheeks. He knew it was too late to make a new batch of challahs. Soon the housewives would come to buy their challahs and there wouldn't be any.

Yossi's father was upset, too. He rushed to pick up the challahs. There was nothing to do but dust them off and bake them. But, what strange challahs they were. Not long and braided anymore. They were fat and round.

As soon as the challahs were ready, the first housewife came to the bakery. When she saw the fat, round challahs her eyes opened wide with surprise.

"Do you call that a Rosh HaShanah challah?" she sniffed. "Why, I never saw such a misshapen challah in all my days!" And off she huffed with a fat, round challah in her shopping bag.

The next housewife came. And the next. And the next. Everyone of them criticized the fat, round challahs. The Rabbi's wife came, too. She was as surprised as all the others but she saw Yossi's tear streaked face and said, "My, the challahs do look unusual, but I'm sure they will taste as delicious as ever." She took home two fat, round challahs to serve the Rabbi for Rosh HaShanah.

The Rabbi looked at the challahs on his table. He picked up one. "Hmm, a challah that goes round and round. A challah with no end." He stroked his beard. "You know, my dear," he told his wife, "we hope that everyone will be happy in the coming year. We wish that their happiness will have no end."

The Rabbi and his wife dipped pieces of the challah in honey. The Rabbi took a bite. He said, "A challah with no end seems just right for Rosh Hashanah. A special shape to suit a special day."

The Rabbi's wife told everyone what the Rabbi had said. The people of the little town were excited.

"How wise he is!"
"Round and round. How special!"
"No end, just like our hopes!"
"What a wonderful idea!"

Only Yossi didn't say a word. He couldn't help feeling proud but he made a silent wish that he would be more modest in the coming year.